COOKING
THE
CARIBBEAN
WAY

Copyright © 2002 by Lerner Publications Company

All rights reserved. International copyright secured. No part
of this book may be reproduced, stored in a retrieval system,
or transmitted in any form or by any means—electronic,
mechanical, photocopying, recording, or otherwise—without the prior written permission of Lerner Publications
Company, except for the inclusion of brief quotations in an
acknowledged review.

Lerner Publications Company
A division of Lerner Publishing Group
241 First Avenue North
Minneapolis, MN 55401 U.S.A.

Website address: www.lernerbooks.com

Library of Congress Cataloging-in-Publication Data

Kaufman, Cheryl Davidson.
    Cooking the Caribbean way / by Cheryl Davidson Kaufman—Rev. &
    expanded.
    p.   cm. — (Easy menu ethnic cookbooks)
    Includes index.
    ISBN: 0–8225–4103–3 (lib. bdg. : alk. paper)
    1. Cookery, Caribbean—Juvenile literature. 2. Caribbean Area—
Social life and customs—Juvenile literature. [1. Cookery, Caribbean.
2. Caribbean Area—Social life and customs.] I. Title. II. Series.
TX716.A1 K38 2002
641.59729—dc21   2001001359

Manufactured in the United States of America
1 2 3 4 5 6 – AM – 07 06 05 04 03 02

easy menu ethnic cookbooks

COOKING

revised and expanded

THE

to include new low-fat

CARIBBEAN

and vegetarian recipes

WAY

Cheryl Davidson Kaufman

Lerner Publications Company • Minneapolis

Contents

Introduction

If one word describes life in the Caribbean region, it is variety. In one day, a Caribbean islander might see a flying fish, enjoy an English-style tea party, and dance to the music of a steel band. The Caribbean's many visitors and inhabitants throughout history, from colonists to tourists, have given these islands a rich mix of cultures—and cuisines.

The food of the Caribbean is a particularly diverse blend of tastes and textures that differs somewhat from island to island. Local dishes take advantage of the abundance of fresh foods on the islands, while also reflecting the tastes and traditions of the people who have come to the Caribbean over the years from different parts of the world. Indian curry, Chinese ginger, and the islands' own hot peppers are just a few of the flavors that make Caribbean cooking so uniquely delicious.

English colonists brought these delicious Easter buns to the Caribbean along with other traditions. (Recipe on page 66.)

The Land

The islands of the Caribbean—about thirty large and several thousand small—stretch from Cuba in the north to Trinidad and Tobago in the south. Cuba lies just off the coast of Florida, and there are points on the coast of the island of Trinidad that are only 25 miles from South America.

The geography of the Caribbean islands is as unique as their heritage. Miles and miles of black and white sand beaches line the clear blue waters of the Caribbean Sea. Forested mountains overlook valleys filled with fruit trees, sugarcane, orchids, and ferns. Many of the mountains are active volcanoes. Bright sunny days can suddenly give way to fierce cloudbursts that wash away everything in their paths. Some Caribbean islands are lush and green, and others contain desertlike areas that receive little rain.

Cuba is nearly as big as the rest of the islands combined, while some islands are so small that they are little more than mounds of coral peeking out of the ocean. Overall, the Caribbean is home to about 36 million people.

History

Nearly one thousand years ago, the Caribbean islands were peopled by a variety of Amerindian tribes. These tribes, generally referred to by later European settlers as the Arawak and Carib Indians, had the islands to themselves until 1492, when the explorer Christopher Columbus arrived in the Caribbean region.

When Columbus realized the fortune that could be made from the area's sugarcane and tobacco, he claimed nearly all of the islands for Spain. But it wasn't long before other European countries recognized the riches the Caribbean had to offer. French and English pirates—or buccaneers—overran the Caribbean during the 1500s and 1600s. Many pirates made Port Royal Harbor in Kingston, Jamaica, their home base. The city was often called "the wickedest port on earth" because of the dangerous characters and stolen property that ended up there.

During the 1600s, Spain's power declined and other Europeans began to settle in the Caribbean, including the French, Dutch, Portuguese, and English. The European settlers brought slaves from Africa to work on their plantations. Meanwhile, the native populations had been greatly diminished by disease, and the remaining members of Caribbean tribes had begun to intermarry with peoples of other nationalities who came to the islands.

In modern times, many of the islands are proudly independent of the European countries that once ruled them, although ties still exist between the Caribbean and countries such as Great Britain and France. Independence has brought with it a new exploration of old Caribbean traditions and a strong desire to strengthen and maintain economic and cultural exchanges among the islands.

The Food

The Caribbean islands share a wealth of cultures and traditions. The ancestors of a Caribbean islander may be African, Spanish, British, French, Dutch, Portuguese, East Indian, Chinese, or any combination of these nationalities. Caribbean cooking reflects this rich and varied heritage, while also putting to good use the immense natural resources of the islands, from fresh fish to tropical fruit. The kitchen is the hub of activity in many Caribbean homes, and family recipes are passed down from generation to generation with pride. Special blends of spices, peppers, and other ingredients make each cook's recipes a special treat.

Fruits of all flavors and colors abound in the Caribbean. Mangoes, limes, bananas, coconuts, avocados, breadfruit, custard apples, and akees are just a few of the many delicious varieties. Many Caribbean families have gardens where they grow fruit trees, vegetables, and, of course, delicious hot peppers, or chilies. Some families also grow herbs with a variety of practical uses, such as mint for tea, leaf-of-life for treating coughs, and sinkle bible (aloe) for soothing burns, cuts, and bruises.

Most Caribbean cooks buy the fruits and vegetables they need at open-air markets. Vendors offer callaloo greens, chocho, garden egg (eggplant), potatoes, sweet potatoes, white or yellow yams, taro root, tomatoes, naseberries, otaheite apples, and tamarind. The smells, colors, and textures of these markets guarantee both shoppers and strolling visitors an appetizing experience.

This market stall in the Bahamas displays a variety of fruits and vegetables available in the Caribbean.

Holidays and Festivals

Religion is an important part of life throughout the Caribbean, so many holidays in the region are religious in nature. The French and Spanish brought Roman Catholicism to the islands, and the English brought Anglicanism. In modern times, therefore, Christianity is the

European settlers first brought Christianity to the Caribbean, and Christian churches like this one dot the islands.

most common religion in the Caribbean. However, people who live in the Caribbean observe many other religions as well. Europeans brought laborers from Asia in the mid-1800s. Most of these people were from India, and many of their descendants follow the religions of Hinduism and Islam. A new religion called Rastafarianism has become very popular among people of African heritage, especially in Jamaica.

Carnival, Christmas, and Easter are the year's biggest and most important celebrations throughout much of the Caribbean. The people of the different islands bring their own variations and traditions to each holiday.

Carnival takes place in February or March during the three days before Ash Wednesday, as a preparation for Lent (the forty-day period leading up to Easter). One of the largest Carnival celebrations in the islands is held on Trinidad and Tobago, and people fill the streets with singing and dancing. Festive parades through the islands' towns feature people dressed in bright costumes of feathers and cloth, often in the shape of birds or animals. Performers and onlookers alike dance to the rhythm of steel drums (drums made from metal oil barrels and garbage cans) and other traditional Caribbean instruments.

Street vendors sell all types of food during Carnival, including *pastelitos* (flavored meat or cheese wrapped in plantain dough). Indian foods such as stuffed *roti* (a flat bread) and *polouri* (split-pea fritters) are popular, as is traditional Creole food—a delicious mixture of French, Spanish, and African flavors. Vendors sell dozens of cakes and candies made of coconut, sugar, honey, and condensed milk to hungry festivalgoers. A wide variety of other foods, such as Chinese dishes, roast corn, rice and peas, plantains, and patties can also be found.

Christmas is another big celebration in the Caribbean. Many people begin singing Christmas songs around mid-December, especially in rural parts of the islands. Singing is an especially important activity in Trinidad and Tobago, where competitions are held to find the best Christmas singers.

On Christmas Day, people on the island of St. Lucia enjoy grand holiday feasts. Typical dishes include stuffed baked turkey, sliced ham, pigeon peas, rice and peas in coconut milk, fruitcake, and sweet potato pie. All sorts of cakes, puddings, and fruits are also served. In Puerto Rico, *pasteles*, packets of cornmeal and meat wrapped in banana leaves, are popular Christmas treats. A traditional holiday dish in Barbados is *jug-jug*, a thick beef and cornmeal stew.

In Jamaica many families begin preparing special foods weeks before Christmas. During the holiday season, guests at Jamaican homes are traditionally offered fruitcake, slices of cold ham, and sorrel, a refreshing, gingery drink made from the waxy sepals of the sorrel plant. On Christmas Day, many Jamaicans enjoy sweet potato pone for breakfast. The large Christmas dinner might include turkey, ham, chicken, akee and saltfish, and several kinds of salads and vegetables. Dinner ends with slices of fruitcake or boiled plum pudding.

All over the Caribbean, festivities often continue on Boxing Day, the day after Christmas. People may bring their leftovers to a favorite beach for a picnic, or just spend time at home relaxing and eating with family and friends.

Easter is a joyous celebration in the Caribbean. In Barbados people attend church dressed in brightly colored clothes and festive hats. For the Easter feast, islanders prepare brightly decorated cakes ahead of time. Tables are filled with pork, beef, chicken, or lamb, along with pickled breadfruit, macaroni pie, and rice and peas. Fried plantains, pumpkin fritters, and sweet potato pie are served for dessert, and the food is always accompanied by cheerful conversation, laughter, and fun.

Caribbean islanders also celebrate many holidays and festivals that are not religious, and individual islands have their own national celebrations. The Bahamian Junkanoo Festival evolved from the days of slavery in the Bahamas when African slaves were given three days off at Christmas to leave plantations to be with their families. Modern Bahamians celebrate the festival with African dance, costumes, and music. The festival begins in the early morning hours on Boxing Day and continues through New Year's Day. Bahamians celebrate this joyous festival with parades that display creative floats made of papier-mâché. Musicians with drums, bugles, whistles, horns, and cowbells lead the floats, while dancers in colorful costumes weave in and out of the procession. Vendors serve Bahamian dishes such as fried chicken, potato salad, cracked conch ("sea snails"), and conch delicious fritters.

A colorful parade celebrates the annual Junkanoo Festival in Nassau, the capital of the Bahamas.

Muslim and Hindu festivals are celebrated on various islands, especially in Trinidad and Tobago. In December or January, Eid al-Fitr marks the end of Ramadan, the Muslim holy month of fasting. Mosques (Muslim places of worship) hold special holiday services. Afterward, homes are crowded with the company of family and friends exchanging best wishes, cards, and gifts. Tables are decorated and set for an elaborate feast, and cooks prepare a large variety of vegetarian curries, roti, and other foods.

Caribbean festivals and holidays span a wide range of history and heritage. But whatever the island, and whatever the occasion, these unique celebrations are a great time to enjoy Caribbean culture and cuisine.

Before You Begin

Caribbean cooking calls for some ingredients that you may not know. Sometimes special cookware is also used, although the recipes in this book can easily be prepared with ordinary utensils and pans.

The most important thing you need to know before you start is how to be a careful cook. On the following pages, you'll find a few rules that will make your cooking experience safe, fun, and easy. Next, take a look at the "dictionary" of utensils, terms, and special ingredients. You may also want to read the list of tips on preparing healthy, low-fat meals for yourself, your family, and your friends.

Once you've picked out a recipe to try, read through it from beginning to end. Now you are ready to shop for ingredients and to organize the cookware you will need. When you have assembled everything, you're ready to begin cooking.

The flavors of plantains and pepper make foo-foo *an excellent accompaniment to hearty Caribbean stews and soups. (Recipe on page 53.)*

The Careful Cook

Whenever you cook, there are certain safety rules you must always keep in mind. Even experienced cooks follow these rules when they are in the kitchen.

- Always wash your hands before handling food. Thoroughly wash all raw vegetables and fruits to remove dirt, chemicals, and insecticides. Wash uncooked poultry, fish, and meat under cold water.
- Use a cutting board when cutting up vegetables and fruits. Don't cut them up in your hand! And be sure to cut in a direction *away* from you and your fingers.
- Long hair or loose clothing can easily catch fire if brought near the burners of a stove. If you have long hair, tie it back before you start cooking.
- Turn all pot handles toward the back of the stove so that you will not catch your sleeves or jewelry on them. This is especially important when younger brothers and sisters are around. They could easily knock off a pot and get burned.
- Always use a pot holder to steady hot pots or to take pans out of the oven. Don't use a wet cloth on a hot pan because the steam it produces could burn you.
- Lift the lid of a steaming pot with the opening away from you so that you will not get burned.
- If you get burned, hold the burn under cold running water. Do not put grease or butter on it. Cold water helps to take the heat out, but grease or butter will only keep it in.
- If grease or cooking oil catches fire, throw baking soda or salt at the bottom of the flame to put it out. (Water will *not* put out a grease fire.) Call for help, and try to turn all the stove burners to "off."

- Fresh chilies must be handled carefully because they contain oils that can burn your eyes or mouth. After working with chilies, be sure not to touch your face until you've washed your hands with soap and water. To be extra cautious, wear rubber gloves while handling chilies. Also keep in mind that the way you cut the peppers will affect their spiciness. If you remove the seeds, the flavor will be sharp but not fiery. If you leave the seeds in, beware!

Cooking Utensils

cheesecloth—Gauzy cotton cloth that can be used as a strainer

colander—A bowl with holes in the bottom and sides. It is used for draining liquid from a solid food.

cooking bags—Plastic bags that can be used to hold food while it is being cooked in boiling water

grater—A utensil with sharp-edged holes, used to grate or shred food into small pieces

rolling pin—A cylindrical tool used for rolling out dough

sieve—A bowl-shaped utensil made of wire or plastic mesh used to drain small, fine food

slotted spoon—A spoon with small openings in the bowl. It is used to remove solid food from a liquid.

tongs—A utensil shaped like tweezers or scissors with flat, blunt ends used to grasp food

Cooking Terms

beat—To stir rapidly in a circular motion

boil—To heat a liquid over high heat until bubbles form and rise rapidly to the surface brown—To cook food quickly over high heat so that the surface turns an even brown

core—To remove the center part of a fruit or vegetable

grate—To shred food into small pieces by rubbing it against a grater

sauté—To fry quickly over high heat in oil or fat, stirring or turning the food to prevent burning

scald—To heat a liquid (such as milk) to a temperature just below its boiling point

seed—To remove seeds from a food

sift—To put an ingredient such as flour through a sifter to break up any lumps

simmer—To cook over low heat in liquid kept just below its boiling point. Bubbles may occasionally rise to the surface.

Special Ingredients

allspice—The berry of a West Indian tree, used whole or ground, whose flavor resembles a combination of cinnamon, nutmeg, and cloves

black-eyed peas—Small, tan edible seeds of an herb related to the bean with a large black spot from which they get their name

callaloo—Leafy greens, similar to spinach

cassareep—The juice from the cassava root

cayenne pepper—A hot powder made from chilies. Cayenne pepper is sometimes called red pepper.

chilies—Small hot peppers. Most chilies are red or green, but there are also orange, yellow, and even white varieties.

coconut milk—The white, milky liquid extracted from coconut meat. Coconut milk is available at most supermarkets and Asian markets.

cream of coconut–A thick, sweetened coconut mixture available in cans at most grocery stores

cream of tartar—A white, powdery substance that is sometimes used to give food a smoother texture

curry powder—A mixture of several ground spices, such as cumin and turmeric, that gives food a spicy taste

garlic—An herb whose distinctive flavor is used in many dishes. Each bulb can be broken up into several sections called cloves. Most recipes use only one or two cloves. Before you chop up a clove of garlic, you will have to remove the papery covering that surrounds it.

ginger—A spice made from dried, ground ginger root

ginger root—A knobby, light brown root used to flavor foods. To use fresh ginger root, slice off the amount called for, peel off the skin with the side of a spoon, and grate the flesh. Freeze the rest of the root for future use. Fresh ginger has a very zippy taste, so use it sparingly. (Do not substitute dried ground ginger in a recipe calling for fresh ginger, as the taste is very different.)

kale—A vegetable related to the cabbage with loose, curly leaves

malt vinegar—A vinegar made from malted barley

okra—The small, green pods of the okra plant. Okra is often used in soups and stews, and it can also be eaten alone as a vegetable side dish.

paprika—A spice made from sweet red capsicum peppers that have been dried and ground. Paprika is used for its flavor and its red color.

peppercorns—The berries of an East Indian plant. Peppercorns are used both whole and ground to flavor food.

plantain—A starchy fruit that resembles a banana but must be cooked before it is eaten

saltfish—Dried, salted fish. Usually made with cod, saltfish is available in some grocery stores and many specialty markets.

sorrel—An herb with a tart, somewhat acidic flavor, used fresh or dried

Healthy and Low-Fat Cooking Tips

Many modern cooks are concerned about preparing healthy, low-fat meals. Fortunately, there are simple ways to reduce the fat content of most dishes. Here are a few general tips for adapting the recipes in this book. Throughout the book, you'll also find specific suggestions for individual recipes—and don't worry, they'll still taste delicious!

Many recipes call for butter or oil to sauté vegetables or other ingredients. Using oil lowers saturated fat right away, but you can also substitute a low-fat or nonfat cooking spray for oil. Sprinkling a little salt on vegetables helps to bring out their natural juices so less oil is needed. It's a good idea to use a nonstick frying pan if you decide to use less oil than the recipe calls for.

A common substitute for butter is margarine. Before making this substitution, consider the recipe. If it's a dessert, it's often best to use butter. Margarine may noticeably change the taste or consistency of the food.

Cutting meat out of a dish is another way to cut fat. If you want to keep a source of protein in your dish, there are many low-fat options. Buying lean meat is an easy way to reduce fat. You could also try using a vegetarian source of protein such as tofu (bean curd), tempeh (fermented soybeans), or seitan (textured vegetable protein). These meat substitutes are often sold in the frozen foods or health food sections of supermarkets.

Coconut and coconut products are used in many Caribbean dishes. Coconut is high in fat, but light coconut milk is available at most supermarkets and can be used in place of both regular coconut milk and cream of coconut. However, be sure to sweeten coconut milk if it is used in place of cream of coconut.

There are many ways to prepare meals that are good for you and still taste great. As you become a more experienced cook, try experimenting with recipes and substitutions to find the methods that work best for you.

METRIC CONVERSIONS

Cooks in the United States measure both liquid and solid ingredients using standard containers based on the 8-ounce cup and the tablespoon. These measurements are based on volume, while the metric system of measurement is based on both weight (for solids) and volume (for liquids). To convert from U.S. fluid tablespoons, ounces, quarts, and so forth to metric liters is a straightforward conversion, using the chart below. However, since solids have different weights—one cup of rice does not weigh the same as one cup of grated cheese, for example—many cooks who use the metric system have kitchen scales to weigh different ingredients. The chart below will give you a good starting point for basic conversions to the metric system.

MASS (weight)

I ounce (oz.)	=	28.0 grams (g)
8 ounces	=	227.0 grams
I pound (lb.) or 16 ounces	=	0.45 kilograms (kg)
2.2 pounds	=	1.0 kilogram

LIQUID VOLUME

I teaspoon (tsp.)	=	5.0 milliliters (ml)
I tablespoon (tbsp.)	=	15.0 milliliters
I fluid ounce (oz.)	=	30.0 milliliters
I cup (c.)	=	240 milliliters
I pint (pt.)	=	480 milliliters
I quart (qt.)	=	0.95 liters (l)
I gallon (gal.)	=	3.80 liters

LENGTH

¼ inch (in.)	=	0.6 centimeters (cm)
½ inch	=	1.25 centimeters
I inch	=	2.5 centimeters

TEMPERATURE

212°F	=	100°C (boiling point of water)
225°F	=	110°C
250°F	=	120°C
275°F	=	135°C
300°F	=	150°C
325°F	=	160°C
350°F	=	180°C
375°F	=	190°C
400°F	=	200°C

(To convert temperature in Fahrenheit to Celsius, subtract 32 and multiply by .56)

PAN SIZES

8-inch cake pan	= 20 x 4-centimeter cake pan
9-inch cake pan	= 23 x 3.5-centimeter cake pan
11 x 7-inch baking pan	= 28 x 18-centimeter baking pan
13 x 9-inch baking pan	= 32.5 x 23-centimeter baking pan
9 x 5-inch loaf pan	= 23 x 13-centimeter loaf pan
2-quart casserole	= 2-liter casserole

A Caribbean Table

Every island of the Caribbean has its own traditions and customs, but a common love of food and festivities is shared by all. Families and friends all over the islands enjoy sitting down around the table to share a meal.

However, one of the most popular ways of eating in the Caribbean doesn't involve sitting down at all. The islands have a long tradition of street food—snacks, appetizers, and even entire meals available from the many street vendors throughout the Caribbean. Passersby may stop for a quick bite or linger to chat with other customers as they enjoy treats like jerked chicken (spicy Jamaican barbecue), fresh shrimp, or banana fritters. During festivals and holidays, even more vendors set up shop to tempt the hungry crowds, and no one ever has to look far to find a tasty snack.

A Jamaican street vendor prepares barbecue chicken.

A Caribbean Menu

Below are suggested menus for some typical Caribbean meals, along with shopping lists of the ingredients you'll need to prepare them. These are just a few possible combinations of dishes and flavors. As you gain more experience with Caribbean cooking, you may enjoy designing your own menus and meal plans, from fancy dinners to relaxed picnics.

LUNCH

Callaloo

Foo-foo

Fresh fruit

Fruit juice

SHOPPING LIST:

Produce

1 small onion
1 garlic bulb
¾ lb. fresh spinach or
    callaloo greens
1 medium potato
5 medium plantains
fresh fruit

Dairy/Egg/Meat

1 stick butter or margarine
½ lb. cooked crabmeat,
    canned or frozen

Canned/Bottled/Boxed

2 15-oz. cans chicken broth
1 can (at least 4 oz.) coconut
    milk
fruit juice

Miscellaneous

salt
pepper
paprika

SUPPER

Curried lamb

Caribbean-style rice

Fresh fruit

Banana fritters

SHOPPING LIST:

Produce

1 garlic bulb
1 chili pepper
1 medium onion
2 green onions
2 medium potatoes
2 bananas
fresh fruit

Dairy/Egg/Meat

1¼ lb. lamb shoulder
1 egg
1 stick butter or margarine

Canned/Bottled/Boxed

vegetable oil
1 bag long-grain rice
flour
baking powder
sugar

Miscellaneous

curry powder
salt
pepper
cinnamon

Soups and Stews

Stews and soups make favorite informal meals in the Caribbean, and cooks serve up a huge variety of these tasty dishes. Soups and stews offer Caribbean cooks a chance to be creative and to make good use of whatever is on hand and in season. They may contain vegetables, meat, poultry, or seafood, and just about any other ingredient from olives to okra.

Stews are thicker than soups and are sometimes served over rice, easily providing a full, satisfying meal in themselves. Soups are generally lighter, though still full of hearty flavor. Often served with foo-foo, a bowl of Caribbean soup can stand alone or make up one course of a larger meal.

Cassareep, chili peppers, and cinnamon are among the ingredients that give pepperpot stew its distinctive Caribbean taste. (Recipe on page 36.)

Pepperpot Soup (Jamaica)

This flavorful and filling soup is often served on Saturday, a popular soup-eating day in Jamaican homes.

4 c. water

½ lb. beef stew meat, cut into bite-sized pieces

1 smoked ham hock (about ¼ lb.)

1 lb. fresh spinach with stems removed, finely chopped

¼ lb. kale, finely chopped

5 oz. frozen okra, thawed*

2 medium potatoes, peeled and diced

1 small onion, peeled and chopped

2 green onions, chopped

1 small chili pepper, seeded and chopped

1 clove garlic, crushed

1 sprig fresh thyme, or a pinch of dried thyme

¾ c. coconut milk

1. In a large kettle, bring 4 c. water to boil over high heat. Add beef, ham hock, spinach, kale, okra, and potatoes. Reduce heat to low, cover, and simmer for about 1 hour, or until meat is tender.

2. Pour soup through a sieve to catch the meat and vegetables, with another large kettle underneath to catch liquid.

3. Set meat aside. With the back of a spoon, rub vegetables through sieve into liquid.

4. Add onion, green onions, chili pepper, garlic, and thyme to liquid. Simmer until soup starts to thicken. Add coconut milk and stir well.

5. Remove meat from ham hock, cut into bite-sized pieces, and add to soup. Add beef and stir well.

6. Cook 10 minutes more and serve hot.

Preparation time: 45 minutes
Cooking time: 1½ to 2 hours
Serves 6

*Check your supermarket or grocer for fresh okra in the summertime. If it's available, choose pods that are firm, brightly colored, and medium in size. You can refrigerate fresh okra in a plastic bag for up to three days.

Asopao (Puerto Rico)

This tasty rice-based dish is a relative of paella, the national dish of Spain.

1 clove garlic, chopped

2 lb. chicken (4 to 5 pieces)*

¼ c. all-purpose flour

½ tsp. salt

1 tsp. black pepper

½ tsp. dried oregano

2 tbsp. butter or margarine

½ medium green pepper, cored and chopped

1 small onion, peeled and chopped

1 oz. cooked ham, diced (about ¼ c.)

2 medium tomatoes, chopped

3 c. chicken broth

1 c. uncooked long-grain white rice

1 10-oz. package frozen green peas, thawed

¼ c. green olives with pimentos

¼ c. grated Parmesan cheese

1. In a small bowl, mash garlic with the back of a spoon. Rub garlic onto chicken pieces.

2. In a wide, shallow bowl combine flour, salt, black pepper, and oregano. Roll chicken pieces in flour mixture.

3. In a large kettle, melt butter or margarine over medium-high heat. Add chicken and cook for 8 to 10 minutes, or until brown. Remove from kettle and set aside.

4. Add green pepper and onion to kettle and sauté until onion is transparent.

5. Stir in ham and tomatoes. Cook over medium heat for 10 minutes.

6. Return chicken to kettle and stir well. Reduce heat to low, cover, and cook for 30 minutes, or until chicken is tender.

7. Remove chicken from tomato mixture. When cool, remove meat from bones and cut into bite-sized pieces.

8. Add chicken broth and rice to tomato mixture and stir well. Bring to a boil over high heat. Reduce heat to low and cover, placing a paper towel between the kettle and the lid. Simmer for 20 minutes.

9. Add peas, olives, Parmesan cheese, and chicken and stir well. Cover and cook for 5 more minutes. Serve hot.

Preparation time: 20 minutes
Cooking time: 2 to 2½ hours
Serves 4 to 6

*After handling raw chicken or other poultry, always remember to thoroughly wash your hands, utensils, and preparation area with soapy hot water. Also, when checking chicken for doneness, it's a good idea to cut it open gently to make sure that the meat is white (not pink) all the way through.

Callaloo

This soup, popular on all the Caribbean islands, is traditionally made with callaloo greens. The combination of greens, crabmeat, coconut milk, and spices can make a rich and delicious main course.

4 tbsp. butter or margarine

I small onion, chopped

I clove garlic, chopped

¾ lb. fresh callaloo greens, finely chopped*

3 c. canned chicken broth

½ c. coconut milk

I medium potato, peeled and chopped

I tsp. salt

1½ tsp. black pepper

½ lb. cooked crabmeat (canned, or frozen and thawed)

paprika

1. In a large kettle, melt butter over medium-high heat. Add onion and garlic and sauté for about 5 minutes, or until onion is transparent. Add callaloo greens and cook for 5 minutes, stirring well. Remove greens from kettle and set aside.

2. Add chicken broth, coconut milk, potato, salt, and black pepper to kettle and stir well. Bring to boil over high heat.

3. Reduce heat to low and cover, leaving lid slightly ajar. Simmer for 15 minutes, or until potato can be easily pierced with a fork.

4. Add callaloo and simmer, uncovered, for 10 minutes, or until greens are tender.

5. Add crabmeat and stir well. Cook uncovered for another 5 minutes, or until heated through. Sprinkle with paprika and serve hot.

Preparation time: 20 to 25 minutes
Cooking time: 45 minutes
Serves 4 to 6

*You may be able to buy callaloo greens at specialty or Latin American markets. If you have trouble finding them, fresh spinach makes an excellent substitute.

Pepperpot Stew

Cassareep, which is the cooked juice of the cassava root, gives this dish a distinctive bittersweet flavor. Variations of pepperpot stew are made all over the Caribbean.

1 chili pepper

3 whole cloves

1 2-inch cinnamon stick

2 to 3 lb. chicken (5 to 6 pieces)

1 ham hock (about ¼ lb.)

5 c. water

1 tsp. salt

1 lb. boneless pork, cut into
   bite-sized pieces

1 small onion, peeled and chopped

¼ tsp. dried thyme

1 tbsp. molasses

¼ c. cassareep (optional)*

2 tsp. white vinegar

1. Cut out a 5- by 5-inch piece of cheesecloth. Place whole chili pepper, cloves, and cinnamon stick in center of cloth. Gather cloth around ingredients to form a bag and tie closed with a piece of string.

2. In a large kettle, combine chicken, ham hock, 5 c. water, and salt. Bring to a boil over high heat. Reduce heat to low, cover, and simmer for 1 hour.

3. Skim foam off top of liquid with a spoon and discard. Add pork, onion, thyme, molasses, and cassareep and stir well. Add cheesecloth bag.

*You may be able to find bottled cassareep at specialty Caribbean or Latin American markets.

4. Bring to a boil over high heat. Reduce heat to low, cover, and simmer for about 45 minutes, or until pork is tender.

5. With a fork or tongs, remove cheesecloth bag and discard. Remove ham hock and set aside. Stir in vinegar.

6. When ham hock is cool, remove meat, cut into bite-sized pieces, and add to stew. Stir well and heat for 4 or 5 minutes more. Serve with Caribbean-style rice (see recipe on page 50).

Preparation time: 15 to 30 minutes
Cooking time: 2½ hours
Serves 6

Main Dishes

Caribbean cuisine features a wide selection of main dishes. These might be enjoyed alone for a light meal or with other entrées and any number of side dishes for a buffet or a big supper.

While many of these dishes contain some sort of seafood, meat, or poultry, they also use a variety of local vegetables and spices and are usually easy to adapt to vegetarian tastes. Caribbean cooks are experts at taking simple ingredients and turning them into something special. The secret is skillful seasoning and cooking methods that bring out the flavor in food.

Fish are an abundant source of food in the Caribbean islands. Stamp and go (back) makes a tasty breakfast, and escovitch fish (front) is perfect for a midday meal. (Recipes on pages 40 and 41.)

Stamp and Go* (Jamaica)

These crisp fritters make a special breakfast treat in the Caribbean.

½ lb. saltfish

1 medium onion, peeled and chopped

2 green onions, chopped

1 small clove garlic, chopped

4 cherry tomatoes, chopped

1 chili pepper, seeded and chopped

4 c. all-purpose flour

2 tsp. baking powder

½ c. water

2 tbsp. butter or margarine, melted

½ tsp. paprika

vegetable oil for frying

1. Place saltfish in a medium bowl and cover with water. Soak for about 30 minutes.

2. Drain in a colander. Remove bones if necessary. Place fish in a medium bowl and break apart with a fork into flakes.

3. Add onion, green onions, garlic, tomatoes, and chili pepper and stir well.

4. Stir in flour, baking powder, water, butter, and paprika.

5. Pour oil into a large frying pan to a depth of one inch and heat over medium-high heat for 4 or 5 minutes. Carefully drop tablespoons of batter into oil. Fry until golden brown and crisp on both sides.

6. Remove from oil with slotted spoon and drain on paper towels. Keep warm in a 200°F oven until ready to serve. Serve hot.

Preparation time: 30 minutes
Soaking time: 30 minutes
Cooking time: 30 minutes
Serves 6

*The exact origin of the name "Stamp and Go" isn't known, but one story goes that islanders with a craving for these tasty fritters can hop off a bus, buy a few at a roadside stand, get back on, and go!

Escovitch Fish (Jamaica)

This dish is named for its sharp lemon and vinegar flavor—"escovitch" comes from the Spanish word escabeche, which means "pickled."

3 lb. firm whitefish, cut into
    4 ½-inch-thick slices*

2 large lemons or 6 tbsp.
    lemon juice

2 c. water

4 tsp. salt

4 tsp. black pepper

½ c. vegetable oil for frying

2 c. white or malt vinegar

2 large onions, peeled and sliced

1 tsp. whole black peppercorns

1 chili pepper, seeded and cut in
    strips

1 tsp. whole allspice

1. Place fish in a medium bowl. Squeeze lemons over fish and add 2 c. water. Cover with plastic wrap and refrigerate for 1 hour. Drain fish in a colander and dry thoroughly with paper towels.

2. In a wide, shallow dish, combine salt and black pepper. Coat fish on both sides with mixture.

3. In a large frying pan, heat oil over medium-high heat for 4 or 5 minutes. Use tongs to place fish in oil and fry 5 minutes per side, or until crisp and flaky. Do not overcook. Remove, drain on paper towels, and place in a deep glass dish.

4. Add vinegar, onions, peppercorns, chili, and allspice to oil in frying pan. Stir well. Boil, then reduce heat to low, cover, and simmer 10 to 15 minutes, or until onions are tender. Remove from heat.

5. Pour vinegar mixture over fish, cover, and refrigerate for at least 1 hour. Serve hot or cold.

* This recipe can be made with any firm white fish, such as halibut, cod, or red snapper.

Preparation time: 15 minutes (plus 1 hour chilling time)
Cooking time: 40 minutes (plus 1 hour chilling time)
Serves 4 to 6

Jamaican Patties (Jamaica)

Patties are a Jamaican version of fast food. This inexpensive treat is sold at patty shops all over the island.

1 green onion, finely chopped

2 small chili peppers, seeded and diced

1 lb. ground beef*

1 to 2 tsp. salt

1 tbsp. black pepper

½ tsp. dried thyme

¼ loaf French bread

½ tsp. paprika

1. Place green onion and chili peppers in a small bowl and grind together with the back of a spoon.

2. In a medium bowl, combine onion mixture and ground beef, salt, black pepper, and ¼ tsp. thyme. Mix well with hands.

3. In a large frying pan, break up meat mixture with a fork and cook over medium-low heat until meat is barely browned. Remove pan from heat and drain off fat.

4. Place bread in a medium saucepan and cover with cold water. Let soak for 5 minutes, then squeeze out and save water. Place bread in a medium bowl and grind with the back of a spoon.

5. Return bread to soaking water. Add remaining thyme and stir. Cook over medium heat until no liquid remains.

6. Add bread and paprika to meat mixture and mix well. Cook over low heat for 20 minutes. Remove from heat and set aside to cool.

While beef is the most common filling, these patties can also be filled with chicken, shrimp, or vegetables such as potatoes, spinach, yams, or eggplant.

Preparation time: 25 minutes
Cooking time: 1 hour

Pastry for Patties:

½ tsp. salt

½ tsp. curry powder

2¼ c. all-purpose flour

½ c. butter or margarine

¼ c. ice water

1. In a medium bowl, combine salt, curry powder, and 2 c. flour. Rub butter or margarine into flour mixture with hands. Add ice water a little at a time, kneading after each addition, until dough is smooth and not sticky.

2. Form dough into a ball and pat with rolling pin, turning once or twice to make it hold together. If it cracks or falls apart, knead in more water. Wrap in aluminum foil and place in freezer for at least 1 hour.

3. Preheat oven to 425°F.

4. Put remaining ¼ c. flour in a shallow dish. Remove dough from freezer and form a 2-inch piece of dough into a ball and roll in flour. With a rolling pin, roll dough into a 6-inch circle about ⅛-inch thick.

5. Place a heaping tbsp. of meat mixture in center of circle. Fold dough over meat to form a half circle and press outside edge with a fork to seal. Repeat with remaining dough and meat mixture.

6. Place patties on ungreased baking sheet and bake for 35 minutes, or until golden brown. Serve hot.

Preparation time: 1 hour (plus 1 hour freezing time)
Cooking time: 35 minutes
Makes 15 to 16 patties

Curried Lamb (Jamaica)

In the Caribbean, this dish is usually made with goat meat instead of lamb. Depending on the cook's taste, curried lamb can be spicy, mild, or anywhere in between.

1¼ lb. lamb shoulder, cubed*

1 tsp. salt

1 tsp. black pepper

2 cloves garlic, chopped

2 tbsp. curry powder

1 chili pepper, seeded and diced

1 medium onion, peeled and diced

2 green onions, chopped

2 tbsp. vegetable oil

2 c. hot water

2 medium potatoes, peeled and diced

*Make a hearty vegetarian curry by substituting 1 lb. of diced, unpeeled eggplant for the lamb. This also makes a quicker meal—you only need to lightly brown the eggplant in step 2, and the combined cooking time for steps 4 and 5 should only be about 20 or 30 minutes. Be sure not to let the eggplant get mushy by overcooking.

1. Place meat in a large bowl and rub with salt, black pepper, garlic, curry powder, chili pepper, onion, and green onions. Cover with plastic wrap and refrigerate for 1 or 2 hours or overnight.

2. In a large frying pan, heat oil over medium heat for 1 minute. Scrape onions off meat and set aside. Brown meat in oil.

3. Add 2 c. hot water and any seasoning left in bowl to meat and stir.

4. Cover pan tightly and cook over medium heat for 45 minutes to 1 hour, or until meat is tender.

5. Add potatoes and onions and stir well. Cover and cook about 20 minutes, or until potatoes are very soft and gravy has thickened.

6. Serve hot with Caribbean-style rice (see recipe on page 50).

Preparation time: 30 minutes
Chilling time: 1 to 2 hours, or overnight
Cooking time: 1½ hours
Serves 4

Jug-jug (Barbados)

This dish uses cornmeal, an inexpensive staple that shows up in soups, stews, and desserts all over the Caribbean. Jug-jug, popular year-round, is a special favorite in Barbados at Christmastime.

2 c. dried black-eyed peas

½ lb. uncooked corned beef

½ lb. salt pork

I medium onion, peeled and cut in half

9 c. water

½ tsp. dried thyme

½ c. yellow cornmeal

I tsp. salt

½ tsp. black pepper

1. Place peas in a medium bowl and cover with cold water. Let soak overnight.

2. Place corned beef in a medium saucepan and cover with water. Bring to a boil over high heat. Reduce heat to low, cover, and simmer for 3 hours, or until beef is tender. Drain beef in a colander and set aside.

3. Drain peas in a colander. In a large kettle, combine peas, pork, onion, and 9 c. water and bring to a boil over high heat. Reduce heat to low, cover, and simmer for 1½ hours, or until peas are tender.

4. Pour pea mixture through a sieve with another large pan underneath to catch the liquid. Return 3 c. of the cooking liquid to the kettle.

5. Finely chop beef, peas, pork, and onion and add to cooking liquid. Add thyme and stir well.

6. Bring mixture to a boil over high heat. Slowly pour cornmeal into water while stirring constantly. Boil, stirring constantly for 10 minutes, or until mixture starts to thicken. Add salt and pepper and stir well.

7. Reduce heat to low, cover, and simmer for about 20 minutes. Serve hot.

Soaking time: overnight
Cooking time: 5 ½ to 6 hours
Serves 6

Side Dishes

Most of these side dishes have a mild taste and are based on some kind of starchy ingredient. They all make great combinations with spicier main courses, rounding out a typical Caribbean meal, and some of them are standard daily fare. Rice, for example, is usually on the table in some form, either alone or as part of a more complicated dish. Pairing these complementary side dishes with different entrées brings together the many delicious flavors and textures of Caribbean cooking.

These recipes are also simple and versatile enough to be prepared almost anytime. *Akkra* can be eaten as an appetizer, and rice and peas is hearty enough to serve alone for lunch or a light supper.

Akkra, a spicy Jamaican speciality, makes an excellent side dish or starter for a Caribbean meal. (Recipe on page 52.)

Caribbean-style Rice

Caribbean islanders like their rice to be fluffy and tender with all of the grains separate. The secret of good Caribbean rice is to cook it a full 20 minutes without peeking under the lid and letting the steam escape.

4 c. water

1 tsp. salt

1 tbsp. butter or margarine

2 c. uncooked long-grain white rice

1. In a large saucepan, combine 4 c. water, salt, and butter* and bring to a boil over high heat.

2. Add rice and stir well with a fork.

3. Reduce heat to low and cover tightly, placing a paper towel between saucepan and lid. Cook for about 20 minutes, or until all liquid has been absorbed. Do not open lid before 20 minutes have passed.

4. Fluff rice with a fork, place in a serving dish, and serve immediately.

Preparation and cooking time: 30 minutes
Serves 4 to 6

*For a simple variation on basic rice, try adding about 1½ tsp. of curry powder with the salt and butter. This easy step will add some spice!

Rice and Peas

Rice and peas, a dish that is just as tasty eaten by itself as it is served with meat and gravy, is a favorite in homes throughout the Caribbean.

1 c. dried red kidney beans*

4 c. coconut milk

1 clove garlic, chopped

2 green onions

3 sprigs fresh thyme, finely chopped, or ¼ tsp. dried thyme

1 tsp. salt

½ tsp. black pepper

3 c. water

3 c. uncooked long-grain white rice

1. Place beans in a colander and rinse well with cold water.

2. In a large saucepan, combine beans with enough water to cover them, then add coconut milk and garlic. Bring to a boil over high heat. Reduce heat to low and cover, leaving lid slightly ajar. Simmer for about 1½ hours, or until beans are tender. Do not overcook.

3. Add green onions, thyme, salt, black pepper, 3 c. water, and rice. Bring to a boil over high heat. Reduce heat to low and cover tightly, placing a paper towel between saucepan and lid. Simmer for 20 minutes.

4. Remove cover and stir gently with a fork. Rice grains should be separate and fluffy, and water should be absorbed. If not, cover and continue to cook, checking every 5 minutes until done.

*In the Caribbean, beans are usually called peas.

Preparation time: 15 minutes
Cooking time: 2 to 2½ hours
Serves 6 to 8

Akkra (Jamaica)

Lots of chili peppers give this simple dish quite a kick!

2 c. dried black-eyed peas

6 chili peppers*

⅓ c. water

vegetable oil for frying

1. Place peas in a large saucepan and cover with water. Let soak overnight.

2. Rub peas together between your palms to remove and discard skins (it may help to rinse peas off).

3. Place peas in a blender, 1 c. at a time, and blend about 20 seconds until smooth. Remove ground peas from blender, place in a large bowl, and repeat with remaining peas.

4. Cut chili peppers in half. Remove and discard stems and seeds. Place peppers in blender and blend about 20 seconds.

5. Add ground chili peppers to peas and stir. If mixture is dry, stir in water, little by little, until pasty. Beat with a spoon until light and fluffy.

6. Pour 1 inch of oil into a large frying pan and heat for 4 or 5 minutes over medium-high heat. Carefully drop rounded tbsp. of pea mixture into oil and fry 2 to 3 minutes per side, or until golden brown. Remove from oil with slotted spoon and drain on paper towels.

*Hot peppers range in spiciness, from poblano and cascabel peppers, near the bottom of the scale, to habañero and Scotch bonnet peppers at the very top. Scotch bonnets, native to Jamaica, are one of the most popular Caribbean peppers. But if you're new to spicy food, you probably want to start with much cooler varieties. Jalapeños are moderately hot peppers and are readily available at most supermarkets.

Preparation time: 25 minutes (plus overnight soaking)
Cooking time: 25 minutes
Serves 6

Foo-foo

Foo-foo, a dish of African origin, makes a tasty accompaniment to homemade Caribbean soups.

5 medium unpeeled green plantains*

½ tsp. salt

¼ tsp. black pepper

1. Place unpeeled plantains in a large kettle and cover with water. Bring to a boil over high heat. Boil 15 or 20 minutes, or until plantains can be pierced with a fork.

2. Remove plantains from water with tongs. When cool enough to handle, remove peel.

3. In a medium bowl, mash plantains well with a fork. Add salt and black pepper and beat with a spoon until mixture forms a thick paste.

4. Roll foo-foo into 1½-inch balls. Serve with soup or stew.

Preparation and cooking time: 45 minutes
Serves 6

*Plantains are available at some supermarkets and most specialty or Latin American markets. Look for large, firm plantains that are greenish yellow in color. To peel plantains, use a sharp knife to cut off both ends and carefully slit the skin lengthwise. You should be able to remove the rest of the peel with your fingers.

Desserts

In the Caribbean, a typical meal is more likely to end with a simple piece of fresh fruit than a rich chocolate concoction. A delicious variety of fruit is available on the islands, from pineapples and bananas to the more exotic mangoes, papayas, and custard apples.

However, Caribbean cooks do make a range of traditional desserts, particularly for special occasions. Cakes, tarts, and other pastries, many of them British in origin, are popular on holidays. Desserts made with fruit, including different kinds of pudding, sherbet, and ice cream, are also favorites. The following recipes offer a sampling of Caribbean sweets.

For a rich, delicious treat, try duckunoo—a perfect combination of raisins, molasses, cinnamon, and brown sugar. (Recipe on page 57.)

Coconut Ice (Barbados)

This sweet and icy coconut treat is the perfect dessert on a hot Caribbean night.

2 c. whole milk*

3 c. shredded coconut

1 c. sugar

pinch cream of tartar

1 egg yolk, beaten

2–3 drops almond extract

To lower the fat content of coconut ice, substitute 2% milk for whole milk.

1. In a small saucepan, scald milk. Place 2 c. coconut in a sieve. Pour hot milk over coconut while holding sieve over large bowl to catch liquid. Use the back of a spoon to squeeze all of the milk out of the coconut.

2. In a large saucepan, combine coconut milk (extracted in Step 1), sugar, and cream of tartar. Cook over low heat, stirring constantly, until sugar has dissolved.

3. Remove pan from heat and add beaten egg yolk (use an egg separator to isolate the yolk). Beat well with a spoon. Stir in remaining 1 c. shredded coconut and add 2 or 3 drops almond extract.

4. Pour into 2 pie pans. Cover with plastic wrap and place in freezer.

5. Remove coconut ice from freezer after 4 hours and break apart with a fork. Serve immediately.

Preparation time: 10 minutes
Cooking time: 25 minutes
Freezing time: 4 hours
Serves 4 to 6

Duckunoo (Jamaica)

Duckunoo is sometimes called tie-a-leaf because the dough was traditionally cooked in banana leaves.*

3½ c. yellow cornmeal

1½ c. dark brown sugar

1 tsp. cinnamon

½ tsp. allspice

¼ tsp. salt

1½ c. coconut milk

2 tsp. molasses

1 tsp. vanilla extract

⅓ c. raisins

*If you'd like to try the traditional method, look for frozen banana leaves at specialty markets that sell Latin American, African, or Asian foods. Using pieces of thawed leaves about six inches square, drop dough onto the center of each leaf and fold up the corners to make tight bundles. (It may help to warm the leaves slightly before using.) Tie the packages with cord or string and follow the cooking directions above.

1. In a large bowl, combine cornmeal, brown sugar, cinnamon, allspice, and salt.

2. In a medium bowl, combine coconut milk, molasses, vanilla extract, and raisins.

3. Add coconut milk mixture to dry ingredients and stir well. Mixture should have the consistency of thick cookie dough. Stir in a few drops of water to thin if necessary.

4. Drop about 2 tbsp. of dough into a cooking bag, twist bag closed, and secure with a rubber band or string. Repeat with remaining dough.

5. Fill a large kettle half full of water and boil over high heat. Carefully drop bags into boiling water and reduce heat to medium-high. Cover, leaving lid slightly ajar to let steam escape. Boil gently for 1½ hours, or until mixture is firm.

6. With a slotted spoon, remove bags from water. Dry off bags and unwrap duckunoo. Serve warm or cold.

Preparation time: 30 minutes
Cooking time: 1½ hours
Makes 12 to 14 bags

Banana Fritters

These sweet Caribbean fritters are delicious served with cream of coconut for dipping.

2 large ripe bananas, mashed

3 tbsp. plus 1 tsp. all-purpose flour

½ tsp. baking powder

4 tbsp. sugar

dash cinnamon

1 egg, beaten

vegetable oil for frying*

1. In a medium bowl, combine bananas, flour, baking powder, 2 tbsp. sugar, cinnamon, and egg and stir well.

2. Pour oil into a large frying pan to a depth of ½ inch. Heat over medium-high heat for 4 or 5 minutes.

3. Carefully drop tbsp. of dough into oil and fry for 2 or 3 minutes per side, or until golden brown.

4. With a slotted spoon, carefully remove fritters from oil and drain on paper towels. Sprinkle with remaining sugar and serve hot.

Preparation time: 15 minutes
Cooking time: 25 to 30 minutes
Makes 12 fritters

*For a lighter version of banana fritters, you can cook them without oil in a nonstick pan. Fry lightly until golden brown, using a spatula to flip them occasionally.

Banana fritters can be served either as a special breakfast food or as a dessert.

Holiday and Festival Food

No Caribbean celebration would be complete without lots of delicious food for all to share. Holiday or festival food in the islands can range from an enormous feast at home to a quick snack at a street stand, but it's always sure to be enjoyed in the good company of family and friends.

Like the rest of Caribbean cuisine, the food eaten on special occasions reflects both the wide range of outside influences on the islands and the rich variety of native tastes and ingredients. Prepare the following recipes for holidays or year-round to bring a festive taste of the Caribbean to your kitchen.

In the Caribbean, a breakfast of sweet potato pone makes Christmas morning extra special. (Recipe on page 63.)

Boiled Corn (Trinidad and Tobago)

Carnival is celebrated all over the Caribbean, but the largest celebration is in Trinidad and Tobago. Corn is a popular Carnival food, and boiled corn is a favorite.

6 ears of corn, shucked

2 onions, chopped

2 cloves of garlic, chopped

3 chives, chopped

I sprig of fresh thyme, whole

I chili pepper, seeded and finely chopped*

I tbsp. sweet (unsalted) butter

salt and pepper to taste

1. Combine all ingredients in a pot with enough water to cover the corn. Bring to a boil. Boil for 5 minutes and remove from heat.

2. Remove ears of corn from pot. Serve with salt and pepper to season.

Preparation time: 15 minutes
Cooking time: 15 minutes
Serves 6

For spicier corn, add another chili pepper. Or, for brave diners, serve with cayenne pepper for sprinkling on corn.

Sweet Potato Pone (Barbados and Jamaica)

Sweet potato pone is a Christmas morning tradition in many Caribbean households.

1 lb. raw sweet potatoes, peeled and grated (about 1⅔ c. packed)

1 c. whole milk

1 c. cream of coconut

1¼ to 1½ c. dark brown sugar

1 tsp. ground ginger

1 tsp. cinnamon

½ tsp. allspice

1 tsp. vanilla extract

2 tbsp. melted butter or margarine

1 c. hot water

1 c. raisins

2 c. shredded coconut

1. Preheat oven to 375°F.

2. In a large bowl, combine sweet potatoes, milk, cream of coconut, 1¼ c. brown sugar, ginger, cinnamon, allspice, and vanilla extract.

3. Add melted butter, 1 c. hot water, raisins, and coconut and stir well.

4. Taste mixture for sweetness and add more brown sugar if desired.

5. Pour into greased 3-qt. casserole dish. Bake for about 1 hour, or until mixture is firm in the middle. Serve warm.

Preparation time: 40 to 45 minutes
Cooking time: 1 hour
Serves 6

Sorrel (St. Lucia and Jamaica)

Sorrel is a popular drink all year long, but households on St. Lucia make and bottle massive amounts of it to be served at Christmastime.

9 oz. dried sorrel*

½ oz. grated ginger root

dried orange peel from about half an orange

1 whole clove

4 c. water

⅔ c. sugar, more to taste

1. Place sorrel in a mixing bowl and add ginger, orange peel, and clove.

2. Boil water and carefully pour it into the bowl.

3. Add sugar and mix well. Let mixture sit overnight.

4. Pour mixture through a sieve with another bowl underneath to catch the liquid. Taste and add more sugar if necessary. Serve over ice.

Preparation time: 30 minutes
Waiting time: overnight
Serves 5

*Dried sorrel is available at most Asian, African, or Latin American food stores. You may find more than one variety, but red sorrel is a popular choice for the holidays.

Deep red sorrel is a festive—and tasty—addition to a holiday table.

Easter Buns

When the English came to the Caribbean, they brought along these traditional Easter treats.

1¼-oz. package active dry yeast
   (about 1 tbsp.)

⅓ c. packed brown sugar

½ tsp. salt

1 tsp. ground cinnamon

1 tsp. nutmeg

4 c. all-purpose flour

¼ c. butter

1 c. milk

2 eggs

½ c. raisins

¼ c. chopped red candied cherries

½ egg mixed with 1 tbsp. milk

¼ c. powdered sugar

2 tsp. water

1. Mix yeast, sugar, salt, cinnamon, and nutmeg with 1 c. flour in large bowl.

2. Melt butter in a small saucepan. Add milk and heat until very warm. Add this to flour mixture and beat until smooth.

3. Add eggs and 1 c. flour. Beat until very smooth and scrape down side of bowl. Gradually add rest of flour until a soft dough is formed.

4. Turn dough onto floured board. Knead until smooth and elastic, about 10 minutes.

5. Grease a large bowl. Place dough in greased bowl, turning it once to coat the surface. Cover and let rise 1 hour in a warm place, until dough doubles in size.

6. Punch down dough. Add raisins and cherries, kneading to distribute them throughout dough. Divide dough into halves, then shape each half into an 8-inch square.

7. Cut each square into 9 pieces. Place buns in greased muffin tins, cover and let rise in a warm place for 1 hour.

8. Preheat oven to 375°F. While oven is heating, lightly cut a cross in top of each bun and brush with egg-milk mixture. Bake 15 to 20 minutes, or until brown.

9. While buns are baking, mix powdered sugar and 2 tsp. water in a small bowl. Brush mixture onto buns after they have been removed from the oven but are still slightly warm.

Preparation time: 1 hour (plus rising time of 2 hours)
Baking time: 15 to 20 minutes
Makes 18 buns

Bahamian Potato Salad (Bahamas)

Bahamians celebrate the Junkanoo Festival from December 26 (Boxing Day) through New Year's Day with African dance, costumes, and music.

1 lb. potatoes, peeled and chopped into ½-inch cubes

5 oz. mayonnaise*

1 oz. mustard

¼ tsp. lime juice

¼ tsp. hot red pepper, finely diced

salt and black pepper to taste

2 onions, finely chopped

2 celery stalks, finely chopped

2 green peppers, finely chopped

2 eggs, hard-boiled (boiled for about 10 minutes) and chopped into ½-inch cubes

2 cloves of garlic, finely chopped

1. Cook the potatoes in salted water for 25 minutes, or until soft. Drain and allow to cool.

2. Mix mayonnaise, mustard, lime juice, red pepper, salt, and black pepper. Add potatoes and stir well to coat.

3. Stir in onion, celery, green pepper, eggs, and garlic. Mix well and serve.

Preparation time: 45 minutes
Cooking time: 25 minutes
Serves 4

*To lower the fat content of this creamy salad, try substituting plain yogurt for mayonnaise.

Bahamian potato salad is usually served as a side dish or complement to other main courses enjoyed during the Junkanoo Festival.

Index

About the Author

Cheryl Davidson Kaufman was born and raised in Kingston, Jamaica. After attending college in Indiana, she moved to Minnesota, where she managed a hospital cafeteria and played keyboards with several reggae bands.

Kaufman learned to cook from her grandmother, mother, and aunts, a group she considered to be "some of the best from-scratch cooks in the Caribbean." She grew up loving to spend time in the kitchen, trying new recipes and experimenting with Caribbean and other types of cooking.

Photo acknowledgements
The photographs in this book are reproduced courtesy of: © Joan Iaconetti, pp. 2–3, 15; © Walter, Louiseann Pietrowicz/September 8th Stock, pp. 4 (both), 5 (both), 6, 16, 28, 31, 34, 48, 54, 60, 65, 69; © Robert Fried, p. 11; © Layne Kennedy/Corbis, p. 12; © Eye Ubiquitous/Corbis, p. 24; © Robert L. & Diane Wolfe, pp. 38, 45, 59.

Cover photos: © Robert L. & Diane Wolfe, front top; © Walter, Louiseann Pietrowicz/September 8th Stock, front bottom, spine, and back.

The illustrations on pp. 7, 8, 17, 25, 29, 30, 32, 35, 36, 39, 40, 41, 42, 44, 49, 50, 51, 52, 53, 55, 56, 58, 61, 62, 64, 68 and the map on p. 8 are by Tim Seeley.